Simple SUPERNATURAL

Simple SUPERNATURAL

KEYS TO LIVING IN THE GLORY REALM

JOSHUA S. MILLS

Published by XP Publishing
A department of Christian Services Association
P.O. Box 1017, Maricopa, Arizona 85139
United States of America
www.XPpublishing.com

ISBN 13: 978-1-936101-19-1
ISBN 10: 1-936101-19-X

Printed in Canada. For worldwide distribution.

Endorsements

I believe that everything pertaining to the Kingdom is simple to understand and easy to engage in. Jesus taught that to enter the Kingdom you must come as a child... and children need it SIMPLE! Joshua is a seasoned minister in the glory and the supernatural. Any time I have opportunity to sit at the feet of Jesus through Joshua's ministry, I do. I am absolutely confident that you will not only receive vital understanding of the supernatural through this God-appointed project, but you will also receive impartation to live in the simplicity of it. I fully endorse this project and the reliable, God-honoring, ministry of Joshua Mills.

Patricia King
Co-Founder, XPmedia
Maricopa, Arizona

I am excited to share with you Joshua Mills' book *Simple Supernatural.* I have ministered together with Joshua, I have spent personal time in fellowship with him and his beautiful family, and I have witnessed the extraordinary supernatural power that flows through his life. Impartation is given not only by what we speak but by what we live. Joshua lives in the supernatural glory realms of God. His life stories and revelations of truth found in this book will inspire you to live a supernatural life that will release God's power in and through you every where you go.

Matt Sorger
Host of TV's Power for Life
Matt Sorger Ministries
Selden, New York

This was such a great read! I love Joshua's testimonies of the simple supernatural – so faith building! Joshua's hunger for the fullness of the Kingdom, His passion for souls and tangible revelation is insightful and infectious. I have already been putting some things I learned to work! Thanks, Joshua. You continue to inspire us to simply live "the stuff."

FAYTENE KRYSKOW,
REVIVALIST AND LEADER
OF THECRY/MY CANADA

In every generation new voices are raised up that bring forth age-old truths in relevant and fresh packages. The key to impact with these next-generation vessels is to be Jesus centered, biblically grounded, relationally accountable and to operate with a now word. Joshua and Janet Mills are two of the shining lights for whom the Word is their very life and whose life is Supernaturally anointed. *Simple Supernatural* contains keys so that you, too, can be a contagious carrier of God's divine purpose.

JAMES W. GOLL
ENCOUNTERS NETWORK
AUTHOR OF *THE SEER*, *PRAYER STORM*,
THE COMING ISRAEL AWAKENING,
AND MANY OTHERS
FRANKLIN, TENNESSEE

If anyone is qualified to write a book on the supernatural it is Joshua Mills. He and his family live in the real realm of the supernatural. Joshua is a man before his time, called and anointed by God with unusual signs and wonders. I have ministered with him and witnessed these signs and wonders first hand, and must say they are astounding to the natural mind and eye. But what is more astounding to me is to see a ministry so anointed coupled with great humility, integrity and the character of Jesus. I have known Joshua for many years and all I can say is I wish we had a thousand more like him.

Enjoy and receive the tangible impartation from this powerful book!

Chris Harvey
Revivalist & Author
Insights To The Anointing
Chris Harvey Ministries
Brisbane, Australia

This book, *Simple Supernatural,* is encouraging and refreshing. As you read it God will renew your sense of childlike wonder in response to the miraculous power of God as it is released in this world. Hope will rise in your spirit that you, too, can walk and live in joyful victory in the supernatural. Get on the glory train, people, with Joshua and Janet Angela Mills and enter into the *Simple Supernatural*!

JOAN HUNTER
AUTHOR
PRESIDENT OF JOAN HUNTER MINISTRIES
AND HUNTER MINISTRIES
PINEHURST, TEXAS

One of the major success keys I learned both in medical school and neurosurgical residency is that you become who you hang around with. When you expose yourself to Joshua Mills' book, *Simple Supernatural,* don't be at all surprised, after you receive the anointing, when you start witnessing healing with your family and friends. And you can do that without attending even one class in medical school! These Scriptures, along with this awesome presentation, are responsible so that someone like me was able to see more people healed laying hands on them than with the scalpel. You will have the opportunity to fulfill Jesus' Great Commission, which is a commandment, with a mentor like Joshua Mills."

Dr. Phillip Goldfedder, M.D.
Neurosurgeon, Minister
and Author of *Lean God's Way*
Alternative Medicine
Healing Ministry, Inc.
Warrenville, South Carolina

Joshua and Janet Angela Mills have shown me what it looks like to be "simply" surrendered to, dependent on, and loved by a Powerful and Supernatural Father. To have trust, freedom, courage, purity and faith like a child is far more than a worthy aim and desire. This book will help you discover and accept the truths of our place and rights as children of God. I've been challenged, encouraged, and charged, and I believe you will, too!"

Beckah Shae
CCM Recording Artist
Nashville, Tennessee

Joshua and Janet Angela Mills are two of my favorite people in the world. I highly respect their purity, humility, integrity, and faith in God. *Simple Supernatural* is a beautiful book that is able to meet everyone right where they are at and equip them for supernatural ministry. You are supernatural and this amazing simple book will show you how to be activated to bring the name of Jesus much glory!

Jason T. Westerfield
Founder and President
of Kingdom Reality
www.KingdomReality.com
Chester, Connecticut

DEDICATION

To all those who will read this book and put these keys into action... this book is dedicated to you as you go into the whole world with God's simple supernatural, and release His signs, wonders and glory for a global harvest!

This book is also dedicated in memory of my friends and mentors in the miraculous, Charles & Frances Hunter. Their life and legacy continues to live on as the revelation unfolds through the lives of those that they impacted through their anointed ministry.

ACKNOWLEDGEMENTS

I would like to thank everybody that was a part of bringing this book together from beginning to end: Patricia King, Carol Martinez, David Sluka, Ken Vail, Joan Hunter and Hunter Ministries, Zane and Joy Clarke, Partners In Praise and my beautiful family, Janet Angela and Lincoln Mills. This project is a result of your dedicated prayers and support towards me and this ministry.

Thank you!

Table of Contents

Jesus said… "Go into all the world and preach the good news to all creation. Whoever believes and is baptized will be saved, but whoever does not believe will be condemned. And these signs will accompany those who believe: In my name they will drive out demons; they will speak in new tongues; they will pick up snakes with their hands; and when they drink deadly poison, it will not hurt them at all; they will place their hands on sick people, and they will get well."

– *Mark 16:15-18*

Chapter One

You Are Supernatural!

The Spirit himself testifies with our spirit that we are God's children. Now if we are children, then we are heirs—heirs of God and co-heirs with Christ. – *Romans 8:16-17*

When I was in my late teenage years, my pastor often said something that impacted my life forever. Almost every week at church before he began to preach, he would make us hold our Bibles and say, "I choose to believe my Bible on purpose!" What a powerful statement.

I even wrote that statement in the front cover of my Bible!

How often, when growing up, did we hear Bible stories about the children of Israel or the miracles of Jesus, and yet they almost seemed like distant fairy tales recited from a different time and a different place? How often now do we read the Bible and yet fail to realize that this same level of miraculous provision and supernatural encounter is available for us today – at even greater levels!

Jesus Christ is the same yesterday and today and forever. – *Hebrews 13:8*

All over the world there are many Christian believers who don't really believe what the Word of God says. Now, I don't want to sound judgmental when I say that, because I realize that I still have much to learn in regards to living in the supernatural. But, my point is this – we must believe our Bibles on purpose! If we believe what the Bible says, we will do what it tells us to do. If we do what the Bible tells us to do, then we will get the results it says we can have! This is simple supernatural.

Since those early years as a teenager when I chose to believe the Bible on purpose, I have been learning how to walk in the Word of God. I read it and believe it!

As we've ministered throughout the world we have seen the greatest miracles, signs, and wonders released because we have believed God's Word to prosper in us. If you prosper in the Word, it will begin to prosper inside of you!

My wife Janet Angela and I have laid hands on the sick and seen them miraculously recover because the Word of God told us we could do it! (Mark 16:18)

Devils have been cast out and the demonic set free through our ministry because I learned that greater is He that is in me, than He that is in the world! (1 John 4:4)

We have spoken in other languages and unknown tongues because the Word said if we opened our mouth, God would fill it! (Psalm 81:10)

Signs and wonders have become a signature mark of our ministry throughout the nations. Remarkable, creative miracles and supernatural phenomenon are being seen because the Word of God says that signs will follow those who believe (Mark 16:17), and we believe!

STATEMENT OF DECLARATION

I want you to write down the following statement on a piece of paper, and I want you to read it every single day this week. Declare these words out loud to yourself, and begin to believe them in your heart.

I CHOOSE TO BELIEVE MY BIBLE ON PURPOSE!

I BELIEVE THAT I AM WHO IT SAYS THAT I AM!

I BELIEVE THAT I HAVE WHAT IT SAYS I CAN HAVE!

AND I CAN DO WHAT IT SAYS THAT I CAN DO!

I WILL LET THIS WORD BECOME ALIVE INSIDE OF ME...

...SO THAT I WILL BECOME ALIVE WITHIN THE WORD!

As you read and declare these powerful statements over the next week, I believe the Word of God is going to come alive for you in a new way as you begin to read it.

What God Says about You

Look at the following Scriptures and see what God has said about you through His Word:

> ***For God, who said, "Let light shine out of darkness," made his light shine in our hearts to give us the light of the knowledge of the glory of God in the face of Christ.***
>
> – *2 Corinthians 4:6*

> ***We wait for the blessed hope—the glorious appearing of our great God and Savior, Jesus Christ, who gave himself for us to redeem us from all wickedness and to purify for himself a people that are his very own, eager to do what is good.*** – *Titus 2:13-14*

> *"And these signs will accompany those who believe: In my name they will drive out demons; they will speak in new tongues; they will pick up snakes with their hands; and when they drink deadly poison, it will not hurt them at all; they will place their hands on sick people, and they will get well." After the Lord Jesus had spoken to them he was taken up into heaven and he sat at the right hand of God. Then the disciples went out and preached everywhere, and the Lord worked with them and confirmed his word by the signs that accompanied it.*
>
> – *Mark 16:17-20*

The Bible gives us a clear understanding that we are supernatural! YOU are a supernatural *being,* with a supernatural *purpose,* which is to walk in the supernatural *ways of heaven,* while demonstrating God's supernatural Kingdom realities here on the earth!

But you are a chosen people, a royal priesthood, a holy nation, a people belonging to God, that you may declare the praises of him who called you out of darkness into his wonderful light. – *1 Peter 2:9*

The Bible says that we are citizens of another realm. Our true citizenship does not belong to a country of the earth, but we are actually citizens of another country. We are citizens of the Kingdom of God. We are aliens to the earth.

But our citizenship is in heaven.

– *Philippians 3:20*

We are not aliens in the sense that we are trespassing, but we are aliens in the sense that we are invading the earth. The Bible says that we are to be in the world but not a part of its ways. You see, we are supposed to live from another dimension and that dimension is the glory realm. In the glory realm we will begin to produce greater results.

ARE YOU READY?

In this book I want to share with you some secret keys and practical guidelines that will launch you into this simple supernatural lifestyle. As we begin, let me ask you a few questions:

- **Are you ready to win souls in the glory?** The harvest is ready and it's waiting for you!
- **Are you ready to receive and minister the baptism in the Holy Spirit?** This supernatural power explosion is ready for you if you'll receive it and give it away!
- **Are you ready to heal the sick?** So many hurt people are waiting for somebody that will give them hope and bring answers to their problems!

If you answered yes to all of these questions, let go of any preconceived ideas and let the Holy Spirit lead you into the greatest days you've ever known. This is simple supernatural!

Chapter Two

SIGNS & WONDERS

For the Son of Man came to seek and to save what was lost.

– Luke 19:10

We've been experiencing the golden raindrops of God's glory for over a decade now, and I know that there is still so much more for the worldwide body of Christ!

The glory of God is igniting our ability to preach the gospel and see a great harvest of souls come forth. In the past we have relied upon our own natural talents and abilities to bring forth results, but we must learn how to flow in the glory realm. In the glory, God will produce a greater harvest through us as we yield to His Word and His ways.

In one of our recent meetings, Janet Angela and I looked down at our hands and they were glistening with gold dust. This unusual phenomenon has been happening to us for over the past ten years. In times of worship or prayer we will begin to see this golden substance come upon our hands or faces. Just as the Lord sent manna to the children of Israel as their daily provision, so is the Lord releasing this unexplainable sign that represents heaven's prosperity and abundance (Haggai 2:8). Many times as I'm ministering in churches around the world, others will even begin to see this same manifestation come upon them as well. Maybe even as you're reading this book you'll begin

In the glory, God will produce a greater harvest through us.

to notice gold dust coming upon you. The Bible says ***"Arise, shine, for your light has come, and the glory of the Lord rises upon you"*** (Isaiah 60:1). Just as Moses' face began to shine when he encountered God's presence on the mountain, and the Israelites saw God's glory before them as a vibrant flame and a dense cloud – the visible glory of God is appearing to His people in this day and hour.

Even though this supernatural sign has become quite commonplace in our meetings, this unusual manifestation still amazes me each time I see it. This unusual sign makes us wonder! This sign causes us to think about the greatness of God. It turns our attention towards the glory and directs our eyes to Jesus Christ. If the Holy Spirit is able to take nothing and make something – taking the unseen and making it seen upon our hands, clothing, and Bibles – how much more will He do what He has promised to us within His Word!

GOLD REPRESENTS THE GLORY OF GOD

> ***He brought them forth also with silver and gold: and there was not one feeble person among their tribes.***
>
> *– Psalm 105:37 (KJV)*

Within the context of Scripture, gold represents the glory of God. We see this example in the symbolism of the Ark of the Covenant. The Ark was covered with the purest gold and represented the strength and glory of God (see Psalm 78:61). We also see this symbolism in the building of Solomon's temple - the walls and floors were overlaid with gold and also included golden ornamentation. The New Testament tells us that God's temple is no longer one that has been built by the hands of man, but that God has chosen to display His glory through His people (see Acts 17:24-28). We should not be surprised that this glory is now beginning to appear upon us and around us as we minister to Him.

Some people have questioned the manifestation of gold dust because it doesn't make sense with their natural reasoning. Even though we don't fully understand the ways of the Spirit, we accept it as God, because the Bible says that we will be able to discern it by the fruit it bears. We long to see the glory of God cover the whole earth just as the waters cover the sea. The miracle is not about the substance itself; the miracle is where it comes from. It's not about the gold, but rather about a God that delights in blessing His children with gifts from above! He is releasing signs and wonders for the harvest! God is giving us supernatural tools so that we will begin reaping a supernatural harvest of souls in the glory!

God is giving us supernatural tools so that we will begin reaping a supernatural harvest!

A few years ago I was ministering in a church in Brampton, Ontario, Canada. As I was praying and preparing for the meetings that evening in my hotel room, I could sense a great cloud of God's glory being released within me. After showering and dressing in a fresh pair of clothes, taken directly from the dry cleaning bags, I proceeded to the hotel elevator where God was about to meet me in the most unusual and unexpected way!

As the elevator doors opened, I saw three people standing on the lift waiting for me to enter. As soon as I crossed into the elevator, it was as if a dump truck from heaven opened up over my head and covered my entire being with gold dust from the glory realm. Now, I'm not talking about a tiny speck or two. I'm not even talking about clearly seeing it on my face. I mean my entire body looked like it had been completely painted with gold! I must have looked like a golden person because all three people on the elevator began to shout in amazement! These people saw the miracle as it happened in front of them.

I love it when miracles happen this way, as it seems to increase people's faith when they watch God releasing a sign and wonder before their very eyes. This occurs many times as I minister around the world. People are able to watch the gold dust appear on my face, hands, and suit jacket while I preach the Word of God. It is a sign of God's glory! A skeptical lady from South Africa was recently in my meetings in Phoenix, Arizona. After all she had heard, she had come to see me minister since the thought of gold dust falling from heaven seemed too impossible to her (see Matthew 19:26). As she watched me intently from the first few rows, she witnessed miracle gold dust begin to appear all over my face. She repented for her unbelief and left those meetings with a renewed sense of God's joy and love for his people.

God Gives Us Golden Opportunities

Now, when this gold dust began to appear on me in front of those people on that elevator, I don't believe they knew what was happening, except for the fact that it was very unusual!

God truly works in mysterious ways!

> ***"For my thoughts are not your thoughts, neither are your ways my ways," declares the Lord. "As the heavens are higher than the earth, so are my ways higher than your ways and my thoughts than your thoughts."***
>
> *– Isaiah 55:8-9*

The people on the elevator began to shout and make noise, but when the doors closed behind me, I realized that these people were on for the ride whether they liked it or not! God was giving me a "golden opportunity" to reach the lost. Do you believe that God will give you these kinds of divine appointments? I believe He will. I believe He does. I think often times we are just not aware of these opportunities because we haven't spent time listening to His voice. (We have successfully taught hundreds of people how to hear the voice of God through our Intensified Glory Institute training school. If you would like to expand your learning even further, and explore deeper realms of God's glory, I really encourage you to join us at an upcoming school!) When the elevator doors closed, I knew that God was giving me a special opportunity to explain this miracle to the people in the elevator. As I listened to God's voice, He gave me the words to say.

I looked at everyone in the elevator and said, "This is a miracle from God, because Jesus loves you."

Those simple words were all it took to open up their hearts, so I began ministering to them. By the time we reached the lobby level, all three, a gentleman and two ladies, had received Jesus Christ into their hearts. They explained to me that other people

We must allow the power of God's glory to work through us as we go into the harvest.

had shared the gospel with them before, but they had never seen a miracle like this in front of their eyes. They knew God was trying to get their attention.

Signs will confirm the Word of God (see Mark 16:20). We must allow the power of God's glory to work through us as we go into the harvest in the days ahead. We cannot bring in the multitudes with our efforts alone; we *must* be equipped with the power of God to bring forth the lost!

WORSHIP RELEASES THE GLORY OF GOD

Another time, I was ministering to a crowd of homeless people at the El Cajon Foursquare Church in El Cajon, California, during a community dinner that feeds the poor and hungry. I started the dinner with some worship music to bring the Spirit of God into the place. You see, praise and worship music will allow you to tap into the atmosphere of heaven, because as you sing from your spirit it connects with God's Spirit, which allows Him to begin moving in your life.

While worshiping with these homeless people, the Holy Spirit came very strongly. I immediately began preaching the good news of the gospel, sharing with them God's plan for salvation. Just as I began ministering, the gold dust started to supernaturally fall all over the room. This gold dust was appearing on people's hands, faces, and clothing. God's golden glory was raining down with droplets of salvation power! The Bible says that signs will confirm the Word of God. As this manifestation began to occur, I gave an altar call and many responded. This was the beginning of a new life for so many of these beautiful people. They were not only hungry for natural food, but they were also desperately hungry for spiritual sustenance. God is releasing these realms of His glory for the harvest!

God Gives Us Golden Tools for a Golden Harvest

Several weeks ago, as we were ministering at the Pavilion of Victory Church in Camuy, Puerto Rico, with Pastors Tito and Sandra Caban, the Lord released many signs and wonders in the church meetings. Pastor Tito just recently sent us an email saying, "We keep receiving testimonies from the meetings, including mechanic angels that fixed a flat tire on a lady's car and people receiving money miracles. There is a girl that needed a root canal and received a dental miracle while Joshua was ministering."

You know, the wonderful thing about God's glory is that it is always ever increasing! The Bible doesn't say that God will decrease the levels of glory in our life, but as we continue to pursue Him with everything we have, the Scriptures declare that we will go from one degree of glory to the next degree of glory!

During the last night of meetings in Camuy, Puerto Rico, the Lord showered down the heavenly gold dust for over two hours while I ministered to the people. As I was preaching, this gold dust was visibly increasing all over my jacket, on the front of my clothes, and all over my back as well. This gold could be seen sparkling on my face and all throughout my hair – it was absolutely everywhere and it continued to cover me the entire time that I was ministering the Word of God. This was a sign and wonder to many pastors that were in that meeting and to many unbelievers as well. As I was ministering, I could sense the compassion of Christ for the lost and I knew that God was giving us this golden tool for a golden harvest!

The wonderful thing about God's glory is that it is always increasing!

Because of the tremendous amount of visible manifestation, I felt led of the Lord to give an altar call for those who had never received the miracle of salvation. Suddenly the altar area began to fill with precious people that were so dear to God's heart! He had been reaching out to them through His signs and wonders all night – these were "love signs" that carried a greater message than the signs themselves, and now the people were beginning to respond to that call. I asked Pastor Tito to lead the people in the sinner's prayer because I am not fluent in Spanish, and as he did, the Lord came and wiped away many tears – replacing them with joy unspeakable and full of glory!

Miracles like these have been happening because Jesus is Lord and He wants the world to know!

Later that evening as I laid hands upon every person that was present in that meeting, the gold dust continued to appear, falling through the air upon hundreds of people as we watched this sign and wonder raining down directly from heaven. This supernatural gold dust could be seen falling through the air as though the rain of God's glory was watering these fresh seeds of salvation.

Several years ago while we were ministering in Jakarta, Indonesia, our hosts invited us to visit their home so that we could pray with some of their family members. We must have been praising the Lord quite loudly because one of their next-door neighbors stopped by to see what was happening. We quickly found out that he had been suffering with severe pain in his right arm and joints. So Janet Angela and I told him that God would like to heal him and we began ministering to him by laying our hands on his arm. (At this time we were unaware that he wasn't saved yet – but I believe God always finds a way to set up divine appointments!) After prayer the man told us that his arm felt much better and he hurriedly left the house to return to his home. Several minutes later he returned and wanted to know why his arm was covered with a shiny golden substance! The Lord had completely covered his newly healed arm in gold dust from heaven! It was a sign that made him wonder! This gave us yet another opportunity to share with him the goodness of God, and through this encounter, he received Jesus Christ into his heart as Lord and Savior. As we continued ministering throughout Indonesia, miracles like this began happening everywhere we went because Jesus is Lord and He wants the world to know!

SIGNS AND WONDERS INCREASE OUR FAITH

...He showed them his hands and feet.
– Luke 24:40

After the resurrection, Jesus Christ appeared to His disciples. One of the first things that He did was show them His nail-pierced hands and feet. Why did He do this? The Bible makes it clear that Jesus wanted the disciples to see the marks because they were a sign of His eternal love for them. Today the Lord is continuing to display wondrous signs as the Holy Spirit is being poured out all over the earth.

> ***"In the last days," God says, "I will pour out my Spirit on all people… I will show wonders in the heaven above and signs on the earth below."*** – *Acts 2:17, 19*

These signs cause us to pay attention to what God is saying (Mark 16:20), increase our faith, and are tokens of God's love. God's signs and wonders in the earth cause us to focus on the finished work of Jesus Christ and all that He has made available for us in the glory realm. These holy signs cause us to place our eyes on Jesus Christ as He is the Wonder of wonders!

SUPERNATURAL OIL

The first time I experienced the supernatural oil appearing in my hands was when I was ministering as a worship leader at a church in Spring Hill,

Florida. The oil first began to appear as an oily substance in the creases of my hand. Some people would comment that they thought it was just "sweaty palms." But I knew what it was (that it was a gift from God) and I would always thank the Lord for it. I knew that if I could be thankful for the limited measure, I would begin to see the Spirit without measure!

If you will give God thanks for the things He is doing in your life (instead of complaining about the things that are going wrong), you will begin to walk in new dimensions of supernatural power that will cause the manifestation of God's glory to come to you! The Bible says that our thankfulness will open the door to rivers of blessing because we come into His gates with thanksgiving (Psalm 100:4).

The Bible says that our thankfulness will open the doors to rivers of blessing.

Several years later I was ministering at a miracle conference in Rockford, Illinois. The host was a very special man of God who carried a tremendous anointing for healing and unusual miracles. He had a bottle of oil that God had filled supernaturally in the 1970s. The bottle continued to be filled years later and was used to anoint the sick for healing miracles (James 5:14). One night after the meetings as I was sleeping in my hotel room, I awoke because I could feel supernatural oil beginning to flow from my body. This time it wasn't just a small amount appearing in the creases of my hands. It was dripping from my forehead, my hands, and my feet.

This oil continued to flow to such a degree that I placed my hands in the plugged sink and allowed the oil to gather. It was quite overwhelming. The next morning I anointed all the people at the conference with this supernatural oil that I had collected and many people received remarkable healings in their bodies. This was the first time I had ever experienced the oil flowing in such an abundant way. But since that time, the oil has continued to flow as the Holy Spirit desires. Often this oil will come with an indescribable fragrance from heaven.

> ***But thanks be to God, who always leads us in triumphal procession in Christ and through us spreads everywhere the fragrance of the knowledge of him. For we are to God the aroma of Christ among those who are being saved and those who are perishing.***
>
> *– 2 Corinthians 2:14-15*

At times we have likened the fragrance to a "vanilla" smell (this is the aroma of intimacy and is one of the first smells that is often described when entering into third heaven encounters). Other times the fragrance has smelled like frankincense or "cedar of Lebanon" (I believe this speaks of preciousness and strength). Most often the oil will flow with a fragrance that has been described as the rose of Sharon. This is the aroma of the presence of Christ. It is the fragrance of Jesus – He is the rose of Sharon.

Sometimes the oil begins to flow from my hands as I am preaching the Word of God in the meetings. During these times I will lay hands on the sick or release an impartation as the Lord leads. While I was worshiping one afternoon in Coeur D'Alene, Idaho, the oil began to flow from my hands so significantly that I had to place my hands in the hotel ice bucket because the oil had already overflowed two cups. The psalmist David said that "***...he anoints my head with fresh oil, my cup overflows...***" This is exactly what happened to me! I believe that God wants to anoint us all with His miracle power to such a degree that we will be oozing with the love of God and His wonders everywhere we go!

At other times this fragrant oil begins to flow from my feet. There have been times in the glory when I have stood on pieces of cloth material and allowed the oil to puddle underneath my feet, collecting into the cloth as a point of contact for miracles (Acts 19:11-12). Recently while ministering in Ocho Rios, Jamaica, the supernatural oil flowed from my hands and feet to such a degree that the cloths became drenched. I asked all the people in attendance to bring their handkerchiefs, scarves, or jackets as a point of contact and I allowed the oil to flow onto those articles of clothing. We have freely sent these cloths to people who live in every state in the USA, every province in Canada, as well as over 150 nations around the globe. We have received so many testimonies from people stating that they have been healed by the power of God. Family members have received salvation, finances have been restored, the dead have been raised to new life, and extraordinarily uncommon miracles have taken place as they have

God wants you to be successful and He gives you new creative ideas!

used this glory cloth as a point of contact. Praise God for His supernatural power that releases His possibilities in the middle of our impossibilities! Nothing is too difficult for God!

God's Glory Releases Creativity

Did you know that the glory of God always sparks creativity within people? In the beginning, God created, and He is still continuing to create new things through you and me.

Last summer while ministering during the evening meeting at the Full Gospel Business Men's Asia Convention in Singapore, I saw the Lord releasing gifts from heaven upon the people who were present in that meeting. I sensed these were deposits of glory – creative ideas, new inventions, answers to questions, and heavenly downloads. I began speaking and prophesying these things that I was seeing. The next day a businessman from California who was in the meeting told me that he had received one of those heavenly gifts that were deposited the night before. The Lord had answered some questions he had been asking in regards to making his family-owned bakery more productive and the Holy Spirit also gave him a "heavenly download" with a brand new idea for a gourmet line of pastries! God was giving Him new creative ideas for success! Since that time we have received special deliveries of pastries on our doorstep, as this man so generously blesses us with these gifts. We have been able to share them with others and bless several churches and ministries with these special treats!

I believe that God wants you to be successful. The Holy Spirit wants to give you new creative ideas for success! He wants to give you new creative ideas on how to handle your finances. God desires to give you new ideas on how to be a better husband or wife, son or daughter, mom or dad. God will give you new creative ideas on how to worship Him, and

I believe that God wants to give you new creative ideas on how to become a soul-winner in the glory! Read on, and you will learn about a creative idea for soul winning that an angel revealed to good friends of mine.

Chapter Three

SOUL WINNING IN THE GLORY

The Lord is not slow about His promise, as some understand slowness. He is patient with you, not wanting anyone to perish, but everyone to come to repentance.

– 2 Peter 3:9

When I was in my late teenage years, I read a mini-book by world-renowned healing evangelists Charles and Frances Hunter that changed my life forever! It was called *There Are Two Kinds Of...* An angel actually came and sat down with the Hunters, sharing with them a brand new way that they could win the lost!

Since reading that book, I have taken this tool and used it all over the world. Sometimes I have used it in connection with the signs and wonders that manifest in our life, and at other times I have used this tool when we haven't been experiencing any particular manifestation. It works both ways.

I have ministered to many people with this technique and have found great success!

After reading that mini-book, Janet Angela and I became good friends with the Hunters, ministering with them on several occasions at their conferences and healing seminars. I contacted Frances Hunter shortly before she graduated to heaven, and she and her daughter, Joan, graciously gave me permission to reprint a portion of the mini-book *There Are Two Kinds Of...* on the pages that follow.

THERE ARE TWO KINDS OF...[1]

By Charles & Frances Hunter

A simple little luncheon can change your life and it can change your thinking about the way to do things! We were in a restaurant in a very small town in Missouri where you might not expect outstanding things to happen. A gentleman came in and sat down at our table. I still don't know who he is nor where he came from nor who he came with because there were several of us there and he had to leave. Before he left he made an interesting statement. He said, "Frances, I know how much you've always loved winning people to Jesus and I've just discovered a new way and want to share it with you."

---

[1] *There Are Two Kinds Of...* by Charles and Frances Hunter. Published by Hunter Ministries.

We're always interested in learning new ways to win people to Jesus because that's the burning desire of our heart at all times. He said, "As soon as the waitress gets to the table I will say to her, 'There are two kinds of waitresses: those who are saved and those who are about to be. Which are you?'" I was fascinated at the question because it doesn't give you an out!

I instantly recognized it was a "win/win" situation and there was no way you could lose! They are either saved or the only other answer they can give you is, "I am about to be." I am always an "eager beaver" to try new ways, so I said, "Let me try it on the waitress. Don't you do it, let me." When the waitress came up I asked her the question, which has now become so familiar with us at all times, "There are two kinds of beautiful waitresses who work in this restaurant. Those who are saved and those who are about to be, which are you?"

I did not expect the type of reply we got at all, so it was a total and a complete shock! She simply started crying and said, "I guess I'm the last one." God's Holy Spirit beat me to her and He had her completely prepared and hungry! I was holding her hand and I didn't let it go, so I said, "Wonderful! Repeat this after me," and I said, "Father, forgive my sins, Jesus come into my heart and make me the kind of person You want me to be. Thank you for saving me today." She repeated the prayer and once again burst into tears.

I asked her, "Where is Jesus right now?" She said, "In my heart!" She was so affected by her conversion that she had to go into the kitchen for about ten minutes and cry before she could come back and wait on us again! It was really a glorious experience and it taught us something... it is so easy to win people to Jesus in this very simple way. Every person you meet is an opportunity!

Here are some keys to becoming a supernatural soul winner!

1. Set a soul-winning goal. God will meet your faith!
2. Look for the chance to "ask the question." The opportunities surround you!

   Ask the question: "There are two kinds of people: those who are saved and those who are about to be. Which one are you?"

   If they say, "I'm saved" or "I'm the first one," then rejoice with them.

   If they say, "I'm about to be," or "I'm the second one," immediately say, "Repeat this after me."
3. Plant the seed of salvation in prayer.

Have them repeat the following prayer after you:

"Father, forgive my sins. Jesus, come into my heart. Make me the kind of person that You want me to be. Thank You for saving me."

Points To Remember

- Every person you meet is an opportunity. Take advantage of it!
- Don't change the wording the angel gave.
  - Say, "Repeat after me!" If you say, "Pray," you will scare the sinner.
  - After they pray, always ask them, "Where is Jesus right now?" The answer should be: "In my heart!" If their answer is different then have them repeat the prayer after you again.

SOUL WINNING WITH A TELEMARKETER

When I first began using this "Two Kinds of" soul-winning technique, I received a phone call at home from a telemarketer. Usually I tell them that I'm not interested in buying anything, but as I was listening to this lady speak, the Holy Spirit told me to listen to her entire message and then tell her that there are "two kinds of people." So I did as the Holy Spirit asked me to do.

I waited patiently on the phone listening to this lady talk about health care, credit card protection, fitness programs, and long distance phone plans. But at the end of her recited spiel she asked me if I had any questions for her. Now I knew that God was setting her up for something great!

This was a perfect opportunity to open the door and lead her into the greatest miracle that she would ever experience. I told her that, in fact, I did have a question.

I asked her, "Did you know that there are only two kinds of nice people who call my house? Those who are saved and those who are about to be. Which one are you?"

She didn't understand what I was saying, so I repeated myself once more. "Did you know that there are only two kinds of nice people that call my house? Those who are saved and those who are about to be saved. Which one are you?"

I could hardly finish asking my question when the lady on the other end of the telephone immediately said, "I'm not saved and I know I need Jesus!" So, I asked her to repeat after me:

"Father, forgive my sins. Jesus, come into my heart. Make me the kind of person that You want me to be. Thank You for saving me."

Once we were finished praying I asked her, "where is Jesus now?" She responded saying Jesus was in her heart! I told her that she was right and that she could now have a blessed day.

Isn't it wonderful how the Spirit of God will begin speaking to you about creative ways to win souls in the glory? By witnessing to that telemarketer one more soul was added to the Kingdom of God.

SET A SOUL-WINNING GOAL

I have used this soul-winning technique on Pizza delivery boys, flight attendants, waiters and waitresses, and so many others that it is simply outstanding to see the Kingdom results that this will produce. You can be a soul winner for Christ every single day! This is simple supernatural.

The Spirit of God will begin speaking to you about creative ways to win souls in the glory.

When you wake up in the morning, set a reasonable "soul-winning goal" for yourself and see how God will fulfill the desires of your heart. The Bible says that without a vision the people will perish, but the opposite of that is when you have a vision, you will prosper! Many people within the church aren't winning souls because they have not set a vision for soul winning.

Give yourself a goal and watch the simple supernatural lifestyle come alive in your life!

The righteous will live by his faith.
– Habakkuk 2:4

SOUL WINNING AT A HOTEL

Last year while I was ministering in Kokomo, Indiana, I had another excellent opportunity to use this soul-winning technique. As I was getting ready for the meeting one evening, gold dust began to appear all over me in the shower. It was coming from the pores of my skin and also falling down upon me.

When the Lord begins to manifest in this way before the meeting, I always know that He is preparing to do something beyond amazement!

As I left my hotel room and began walking down the hotel hallway, I noticed a friendly couple walking toward me. As the lady looked at me she said "You're really sparkling!" I said, "Yes! This is a miracle from God because Jesus loves you!" She looked at me again in bewilderment and asked, "But how did it get on you?" I was so glad that she asked me another question! Isn't it amazing when God gives us these opportunities to share His love and glory with the world around us? I looked at that lady and said, "Did you know that there are only two kinds of people who ask me that question? Those who are saved and those who are about to be. Which one are you?" She was surprised by my statement and immediately responded by saying, "I guess I'm about to be!" Her husband was looking at her with

God gives us the privilege to share His love and glory with others. Every person is an opportunity!

a glare wondering what was happening… as this all happened so quickly!

I took advantage of this opportunity once again. I looked him in the eyes and said, "Sir, did you know that there are only two kinds of men who stand in front of me like that?! Those who are saved and those who are about to be, which one are you?" And I tell you, the Holy Spirit must have gripped his heart as I spoke those words because he responded by enthusiastically saying, "I guess I'm about to be, too!" Right there in the hotel hallway I led this beautiful couple to know the saving power of salvation through Jesus Christ. I went from that encounter directly into the conference and that night the Lord caused the golden glory to fall and the oil to flow. These are signs for the unbelievers – God is giving us His supernatural power to win the lost!

Did you know that there are only two kinds of people that read this book? Those who are saved and those who are about to be, which one are you?

I'm asking you this question because I believe this book is your divine appointment. You've been waiting for a miracle and right now you're holding destiny in your hands! If in your heart you would say that you're the second one (about to be saved), I want you to say this with me:

"Father, forgive my sins. Jesus, come into my heart. Make me the kind of person that You want me to be. Thank You for saving me."

Wow! Do you know where Jesus is right now? He's inside your heart! The Bible says ***"for it is with your heart that you believe and are justified, and it is with your mouth that you confess and are saved"*** *(Romans 10:10)*.

This is simple supernatural!

Chapter Four

RECEIVE THE POWER!

But you will receive power when
the Holy Spirit comes on you;
and you will be my witnesses.
– Acts 1:8

During the late nineties I was ministering extensively in worship at a revival in El Cajon, California. One night I began singing in the Spirit as the Lord began to lead me into a new song. I started speaking in tongues and ministering under the unction of the Holy Spirit. The evidence of the baptism in the Holy Spirit began to bubble up from within me, overflowing in words and sounds that I didn't understand in the natural realm. It was so wonderful, that at the end of the evening, a little Latin American lady approached me and told me that I had ministered salvation to her in her native Spanish dialect while I was singing in other tongues. In the natural realm I didn't know how to speak her native language. But as a sign for the unbeliever, the Lord allowed me to speak forth words of salvation, directed straight to that lady's heart. It was something completely arranged by the Holy Spirit!

The supernatural realm is not a luxury "add-on" in the life of a believer – it is mandatory!

I will pray with my spirit, but I will also pray with my mind; I will sing with my spirit, but I will also sing with my mind.

– 1 Corinthians 14:15

What a great witness and confirmation to both of our spirits! She left the meeting that evening with a fresh promise of eternal peace, and I departed that church service with a renewed sense of awe for the realms of eternity. As we abide in the glory realm, the Lord will use us to minister in ways that we would have never dreamed possible.

The Supernatural Is a Must

The supernatural realm is no longer just a luxury "add-on" in the life of a believer. It is a mandatory requirement in order to walk in the fullness of God's purposes for us here on the earth.

A few years ago we recorded a live worship CD called *The Drink*. It is spontaneous prophetic worship that the Lord gave to us one evening while ministering at our Winter Camp meeting in London, Ontario, Canada. During this time of ministry, once again the Lord gave me a new song and I began to sing in unknown tongues by the unction of the Holy Spirit. Some time later, when the CD was distributed, I received a letter from an Indian lady who listened to the CD and said she heard me singing in her native Hindi language. I thought this was very interesting because immediately after that Winter Camp meeting in Canada I had traveled directly to Chennai, India, to minister at a revival crusade. Possibly the Lord allowed me to sing in that foreign language as a precursor, releasing declarations beforehand towards the nation of India, for many miracles, signs and wonders to spring up. Regardless, that woman was blessed by this Spirit-led message, and I was once again overwhelmed by the greatness of God's power. This same thing has happened again on several occasions where the Lord has given me various earthly languages as I have begun singing in the Spirit.

THE HOLY SPIRIT RELEASED TONGUES

In the second chapter of Acts, we read about the great power of the Holy Spirit that was released upon the early church, with the appearance of tongues of fire and the sound of a rushing wind. The Bible says that when this power came upon those who were present, they were ALL filled and began to speak in other tongues.

> ***When the day of Pentecost came, they were all together in one place. Suddenly a sound like the blowing of a violent wind came from heaven and filled the whole house where they were sitting. They saw what seemed to be tongues of fire that separated and came to rest on each of them. All of them were filled with the Holy Spirit and began to speak in other tongues as the Spirit enabled them.***
>
> *– Acts 2:1-4*

One of the evidences of the baptism in the Holy Spirit is the manifestation of speaking in unknown tongues. It happened in the upper room and it's continuing to happen all over the world today!

When we receive the baptism in the Holy Spirit with the evidence of speaking in tongues, there are no limitations for what God may do with this new language. The Holy Spirit is able to give you a tongue with foreign languages, ancient languages, future languages, or language only understood in the realms of heaven.

When we begin to pray with this new language, we call it "praying in the Spirit" because the Spirit of God is directing our prayers and intercession.

Tongues Releases Heaven to Earth

One of the greatest revelations of the Spirit is that something is always happening in the glory realm. The activity of heaven is always moving! The cherubim angels, the wheels within wheels, the flashing lightning from the throne, and the whirlwinds of God are moving. So every time we speak in heavenly tongues something is moving from heaven to earth into our spirit man. Heaven is giving us language and creating a new vocabulary of the glory realm within us. These new tongues are even filled with health and healing! Medical science has recently done several studies on "speaking in tongues" and the results are tremendous!

- The brain is proven to be under "divine control" while speaking in tongues.[2]
- As we engage in our heavenly language, the brain releases two chemical secretions that are directed into our immune systems, giving a 35-40 percent boost in the immune system. This promotes healing within our bodies.[3]
- Studies suggest that people who speak in tongues rarely suffer from mental problems. A recent study of nearly 1,000 evangelical Christians in England found that those who engaged in the practice were more emotionally stable than those who did not.[4]

---

2 University of Pennsylvania School of Medicine

3 Dr. Carl Peterson, Oral Roberts University, Tulsa, Oklahoma

4 Dr. Andrew B. Newberg, University of Pennsylvania study team

The baptism in the Holy Spirit releases us into the flow of heaven, opening up the glory realm.

It is a proven fact that we can accomplish a whole lot more when we are moved by heaven's supernatural ability, rather than trusting on our own natural giftings. I'm not saying that our giftings are useless; I believe that God has given us talents, giftings, and abilities. But they must be surrendered to the flow of His Spirit so that they might become vibrantly alive – awakened by the current move of the Spirit.

> ***Everyone was filled with awe, and many wonders and miraculous signs were done by the apostles.... And the Lord added to their number daily those who were being saved.***
>
> – *Acts 2:43, 47*

THE BAPTISM IN THE HOLY SPIRIT RELEASES DYNAMITE-TYPE POWER

The Bible tells us that after the move of the Holy Spirit filled those who were gathered in the upper room, they received a supernatural enablement with signs, wonders, and miracles following, and many people were added to the church on a daily basis. This is what the baptism in the Holy Spirit will do. It brings the enablement to work the works of God. We are hooked up to the power source of heaven through the baptism in the Holy Spirit!

> ***But you will receive power when the Holy Spirit comes on you; and you will be my witnesses.*** – *Acts 1:8*

The baptism in the Holy Spirit releases us into the flow of heaven. It opens up the glory realm for us. The Bible says that when this fresh touch of the Holy Spirit comes upon us, we will receive a dynamite-type power from on high. This explosive power contains enough force to blow out any obstacle of the enemy! Without the baptism we will never be able to live up to our full potential in Christ. We must receive the baptism in the Holy Spirit in order to function as the witnesses that God has created us to be. This is simple supernatural.

In the following pages I want to give you some keys to receiving and ministering the baptism in the Holy Spirit.

When you pray to receive the baptism in the Holy Spirit, all you need to do is ask the Holy Spirit to come and fill you and live inside you with His power. It's that easy. Let me show it to you within the Word of God and give you some practical advice from experience.

The Father Gives the Holy Spirit to Those Who Ask

Read Jesus' words from Luke 11:9-13:

So I say to you: Ask and it will be given to you; seek and you will find; knock and the

door will be opened to you. For everyone who asks receives; he who seeks finds; and to him who knocks, the door will be opened.

Which of you fathers, if your son asks for a fish, will give him a snake instead? Or if he asks for an egg, will give him a scorpion? If you then, though you are evil, know how to give good gifts to your children, how much more will your Father in heaven give the Holy Spirit to those who ask him!

This passage says that when we ask for the baptism in the Holy Spirit, we must rest assured in the promise of God. He is faithful to give us His beautiful Holy Spirit. In other words, when we read this Scripture, we must believe that it is true. And if it is true, as soon as we ask for the baptism in the Holy Spirit, we will receive it. We don't have to wait for another day. We don't have to rely upon another evangelist to minister to us. You can receive this baptism today with the evidence of speaking in tongues! The Bible says that our Heavenly Father will give the Holy Spirit to those who ask for Him!

As I've ministered around the world, I've had people come to me who feel they didn't have a real baptism experience because when they prayed for the baptism in the Holy Spirit, they didn't immediately begin to speak in an unknown tongue. The problem has often been that they expected the results to be almost mechanical and automatic in nature.

Open Your Mouth and He Will Fill It

I want to ask you a question. When you learned how to speak your native language did you keep your mouth closed? I can't tell you how many people have asked to receive the baptism in the Holy Spirit, but then they keep their mouth closed when it's time for them to begin speaking in new tongues.

Have you ever seen a baby that's learning how to speak? That tiny little baby begins to babble all sorts of sounds and noises trying to learn the proper words of speech.

I remember when we were attempting to teach our son, Lincoln, how to speak when he was a baby. I was trying to get him to learn how to say "Daddy." I wanted so badly for him to speak! I wanted to hear him call my name and be able to reach out to me with his vocabulary. As he was learning this new word, he made many goo-goo and ga-ga sounds, until finally he spit out the word "Dadu!" I remember the feeling I had when he first said this. It wasn't completely correct pronunciation, but I loved it nonetheless because he was doing everything he could to say something he had never said before. He wanted to say my name! I loved it so much that I let him continue to use that name. From that time until now Lincoln still calls me "Dadu" and I love it!

So you're asking, what does this have to do with receiving the baptism in the Holy Spirit? When God desires to give us a new language we must open up our mouths in order for Him to fill it. Some people pray for the baptism and then they wait for God to automatically begin moving their jaw up and down, back and forth, articulating the tongue until it says something. Believe me, this is not the way that it happens!

When we pray for the baptism in the Holy Spirit and we BELIEVE that we have received what we have prayed for, we can open up our mouth and trust that God will begin to fill it with his supernatural tongue. Open up your mouth and God will fill it. At first it might sound like a bunch of goo-goos and ga-gas, but as you yield to the Spirit of God, suddenly you will break through into a free-flowing current of heavenly language that has no end!

> ***Open your mouth wide, and I will fill it with good things.*** *– Psalm 81:10 (NLT)*

Here are the keys to receiving and ministering the baptism in the Holy Spirit:

1. You must believe that it is available today! (Luke 11:9-13)

2. Do not believe the lie of the enemy that you're not good enough. The infilling of the Holy Spirit is what will help you live a holy life pleasing unto the Lord (Romans 8:13).

3. Pray to receive the baptism in the Holy Spirit with the evidence of speaking in new tongues.

4. Begin speaking in faith as the Holy Spirit enables you! (Acts 2:4)

Prayer To Receive The Baptism in the Holy Spirit

Father, in the name of Jesus, I thank You that by faith I have received the gift of salvation from You. I believe that Your Word is true and that You have promised me another gift as well – the gift of the Holy Spirit. You have said in Your Word that You would give the Holy Spirit to those that ask. So right now, by faith, I ask for this gift and I thank you for filling me with your wonderful Holy Spirit. I receive by faith this supernatural empowerment from heaven. I believe that I am being baptized in the Holy Spirit just like those who were gathered in the upper room. I thank you for giving me a new language that I may speak in tongues to bring glory to Your name! I believe that I have received this supernatural baptism in the Holy Spirit!

Amen!

Now your step of faith here is to open up your mouth and begin speaking syllables that you don't necessarily understand. This is just like a baby beginning to speak. This is putting your faith into action. You can trust that the Holy Spirit within you will control what you say and make it into a beautiful heavenly prayer language. Sometimes you may only get one or two words at a time. Let the Holy Spirit develop this language for you – it will come word by word, from faith to faith!

The baptism in the Holy Spirit will give you results! Get filled and get ready to be used of God in ways you've never dreamed of before!

You will overcome any doubting or critical spirits that may try to hinder you from this experience by staying focused on the Word of God. Here are some Scriptures for you to meditate upon.

(The following Scriptures are from the New Living Translation).

Isaiah 28:11

O now God will have to speak to his people through foreign oppressors who speak a strange language!

Matthew 3:11

I baptize with water those who repent of their sins and turn to God. But someone is coming soon who is greater than I am—so much greater that I'm not worthy even to be his slave and carry his sandals. He will baptize you with the Holy Spirit and with fire.

Mark 1:8

I baptize you with water, but he will baptize you with the Holy Spirit!

Mark 16:17

These miraculous signs will accompany those who believe: They will cast out demons in my name, and they will speak in new languages.

Luke 3:16

John answered their questions by saying, "I baptize you with water; but someone is coming soon who is greater than I am—so much greater that I'm not even worthy to be his slave and untie the straps of his sandals. He will baptize you with the Holy Spirit and with fire."

John 1:33

I didn't know he was the one, but when God sent me to baptize with water, he told me, "The one on whom you see the Spirit descend and rest is the one who will baptize with the Holy Spirit."

John 7:37

On the last day, the climax of the festival, Jesus stood and shouted to the crowds, "Anyone who is thirsty may come to me!"

John 14:15-17

If you love me, obey my commandments. And I will ask the Father, and he will give you another Advocate, who will never leave you. He is the Holy Spirit, who leads into all truth. The world cannot receive him, because it isn't looking for him and doesn't recognize him. But you know him, because he lives with you now and later will be in you.

Acts 1:5

John baptized with water, but in just a few days you will be baptized with the Holy Spirit."

Acts 1:8

But you will receive power when the Holy Spirit comes upon you. And you will be my witnesses, telling people about me everywhere—in Jerusalem, throughout Judea, in Samaria, and to the ends of the earth.

Acts 2:5-11

At that time there were devout Jews from every nation living in Jerusalem. When they heard the loud noise, everyone came running, and they were bewildered to hear their own languages being spoken by the believers. They were completely amazed. "How can this be?" they exclaimed. "These people are all from Galilee, and yet we hear them speaking in our own native languages! Hadobe jans, Medes, Elamites, people from Mesopotamia, Judea, Cappadocia, Pontus, the province of Asia, Phrygia, Pamphylia, Egypt, and the areas of Libya around Cyrene, visitors from Rome (both Jews and converts to Judaism), Cretans, and Arabs. And we all hear these people speaking in our own languages about the wonderful things God has done!"

Acts 8:14-17

When the apostles in Jerusalem heard that the people of Samaria had accepted God's message, they sent Peter and John there. As soon as they arrived, they prayed for these new believers to receive the Holy Spirit. The Holy Spirit had not yet come upon any of them, for they had only been baptized in the name of the Lord Jesus. Then Peter and John laid their hands upon these believers, and they received the Holy Spirit.

Acts 9:17

So Ananias went and found Saul. He laid his hands on him and said, "Brother Saul, the Lord Jesus, who appeared to you on the road, has sent me so that you might regain your sight and be filled with the Holy Spirit."

Acts 11:16

Then I thought of the Lord's words when he said, "John baptized with water, but you will be baptized with the Holy Spirit."

Acts 19:1-6

While Apollos was in Corinth, Paul traveled through the interior regions until he reached Ephesus, on the coast, where he found several believers. "Did you receive the Holy Spirit when you believed?" he asked them.

"No," they replied, "we haven't even heard that there is a Holy Spirit."

"Then what baptism did you experience?" he asked.

And they replied, "The baptism of John."

Paul said, "John's baptism called for repentance from sin. But John himself told the people to believe in the one who would come later, meaning Jesus."

As soon as they heard this, they were baptized in the name of the Lord Jesus. Then when Paul laid his hands on them, the Holy Spirit came on them, and they spoke in other tongues and prophesied.

Chapter Five

POWER TO HEAL THE SICK

Heal the sick, cleanse the lepers,
raise the dead, cast out devils:
freely ye have received, freely give.
– Matthew 10:8 (KJV)

One of my mentors in the miraculous, Charles Hunter, always said: "Without the baptism in the Holy Spirit we will PRAY for the sick, but with the baptism in the Holy Spirit we will HEAL the sick!" Now that you have received the baptism in the Holy Spirit, you have received the power of God to work miracles, signs, and wonders to bring glory to Jesus!

Through the Scriptures we realize that one of the ways we can utilize this power is to "heal the sick, cleanse the lepers, raise the dead, and cast out devils" (Matthew 10:8). I want to tell you that sickness is a devil! If you've walked through a cancer ward in a hospital or through the streets of India among the lepers, you would say the same thing.

HEALING IS ALWAYS GOD'S WILL

Some people wonder if healing is the will of God. I want to tell you now and settle this issue forever that it is ALWAYS God's will to heal (Mark 1:40-41). Whenever I talk about this, some people say, "Well, if it's always God's will to heal, then why are some people still sick?" It's not our responsibility to answer questions that only God understands; it is simply our responsibility to believe the infallible Word of God. His Word is continually unfailing in effectiveness and operation. We trust it and have faith in it and that revelation will produce a miracle. Do you know the Bible says that a lot of people perish because they have a lack of revelation (Hosea 4:6)? This is why we must find out what the Scriptures say about healing. If we have the revelation we can receive the manifestation.

Without God's Word on healing, the enemy will always lie to us and try to make us believe that we must be sick (see John 10:10). Some others say, "Sister So-And-So was such a good Sunday school teacher. She faithfully played piano at church and she never missed a meeting. So why is she still sick?" I want to say that our healing never depends upon what we have done, but it is a completed work that was finished by Jesus Christ at the cross of Calvary. In other words, healing is something we can receive because of what He's done! If we believe it, we'll receive it!

Healing is something we can receive because of what He's done!

Sickness Is Never the Work of God

Sickness is never the work of God. Sickness is always the work of the devil. But praise God that with the baptism in the Holy Spirit, we have the authority and power over every work of the devil (Luke 10:19)!

> ***When evening came, many who were demon-possessed were brought to him, and he drove out the spirits with a word and healed all the sick. This was to fulfill what was spoken through the prophet Isaiah: "He took up our infirmities and carried our diseases."***
>
> *– Matthew 8:16-17*

The Bible says that when Jesus Christ was here on the earth He walked in this miraculous power to heal the sick. He opened up deaf ears (Mark 7:32-37), told the lame man to walk (Matthew 9:2-8), and at his command, the withered hand became strengthened (Luke 6:6-10). He caused blind eyes to regain their sight (Matthew 20:29-34), raised the dead (Luke 7:12-16), and healed a woman that had been suffering for eighteen years with a serious infirmity (Luke 13:10-17). These are just a few of the many many miracles He did.

> ***And Jesus went about all the cities and villages, teaching in their synagogues, and preaching the gospel of the Kingdom, and healing every sickness and every disease among the people.*** *– Matthew 9:35 (KJV)*

Jesus Is Our Example

I want us to look once again at that Scripture. I want you to clearly see what Jesus did and how He operated in this miraculous ministry, because He is our ultimate example. We can learn how to operate in this realm of glory as we pay attention to His methods and His ways.

Jesus Was Teaching

> ***And Jesus went about all the cities and villages, teaching in their synagogues.***
>
> *– Matthew 9:35 (KJV)*

We can begin walking in supernatural demonstration by teaching the Word.

The Bible says that as Jesus traveled through cities and villages He taught the people. What did Jesus teach the people in their synagogues? I believe He began teaching them the will of God, which is the Word of God. Teaching is always systematic – the revelation is revealed line upon line, precept upon precept (Isaiah 28:10). So we find a key here within the Scriptures that one of the ways we can begin walking in supernatural demonstration is by teaching the Word. You can do this by speaking the Word of God into every situation of sickness, illness, or infirmity that you encounter.

At one of our recent Intensified Glory Institutes we were ready to demonstrate the power of God for healing the sick while I was teaching a class on "How To Operate In Creative Miracles." I began to read many healing Scriptures from both the Old Testament and the New Testament. There was a man in the class who had been suffering with a constant buzzing in his ears for over twenty years; it had never stopped for even a day during that time. But as I read the Word of God in regard to healing, suddenly the buzzing instantly stopped and this man could hear once again with clarity. The Word of God is a healing Word! As you teach and preach the Word of God, it releases faith for that which is being spoken.

Through the Intensified Glory Institute we have received hundreds of testimonies of supernatural healings that have taken place instantly as the Word of God was taught – and the revelation was caught!

The Scriptures declare that faith comes by the hearing of the Word! In other words, there is not one person on earth who cannot receive the healing power of God into their situation – because even if they feel as though they don't have the "faith for it", the Bible declares that the necessary faith will come as we hear God's perspective on the situation by listening to His Word. This is why it is so important for us to be diligent about reading the Word of God and speaking His Word.

JESUS WAS PREACHING

> ***...and preaching the gospel of the Kingdom...*** *– Matthew 9:35 (KJV)*

The next thing we need to notice about this passage of Scripture is that Jesus was preaching the good news of the Kingdom! What is this good news? What is this message that comes from God's heavenly Kingdom?

- In the Kingdom there is no sickness or disease! (Revelation 21:4)
- In the Kingdom there is no pain, sorrow, or suffering! (Revelation 7:17)
- In the Kingdom there is no more death! (Luke 20:36)

Preaching is not always systematic in nature as teaching is, but many times it is more prophetic in that it comes by inspiration. We become inspired to preach! You may feel there is no way that you could ever be inspired to preach. Well, let me explain it like this… you don't need a microphone in your hand, or a pulpit in front of you, or even a congregation gathered to hear you in order for you to preach. As you begin to learn how to live in the realms of glory, you will find that every day you're surrounded with people and opportunities where you are given the ability to speak "prophetically" into the lives of others. Jesus preached this good news of the Kingdom and He began to get the results of the Kingdom!

Let God inspire you to speak His Word into the lives of others. When you see someone who is hurting, allow the Holy Spirit to give you words of comfort and healing. These words can become prophetic in the sense that you can change somebody's situation by the atmosphere you create with your words! Jesus did!

The healing power of God's Holy Spirit was released as Jesus began to teach and preach to the people!

When Janet Angela and I first came into understanding these Kingdom truths about God's healing power, we felt as though we had been electrified with a lightning bolt from heaven – and in essence, we had! Around that time we were ministering in a series of revival meetings at a Baptist church in Florida. There was a lady in those meetings who had been born without an eardrum in her left ear. She had grown up and lived her entire life believing that this was the way it was always going to be. You see, faith for the miraculous cannot come until you hear the Word. This is why it is important to teach

The healing power of God's Holy Spirit was released as Jesus began to teach and preach!

and preach God's Word in order that faith would arise for the impossible!

In the altar area, Janet Angela and I began to speak God's Word concerning healing to this woman. As we did, her face lit up and it was as though the lights came on for her with the revelation of God's healing power! After teaching the Word to her (by simply speaking the Word), I began to preach the Kingdom as I prophesied to her body and commanded a new eardrum to form. Instantly, Janet Angela placed her hand over the lady's good ear and began speaking into the ear that had been without an eardrum. Do you know what happened? A brand new eardrum had formed inside her ear! For the first time in this lady's life she was actually able to hear from that side of her head!

It was only a matter of minutes from beginning to end, but in the simplicity of believing the Word – teaching it, preaching it, and demonstrating it – that woman's life was changed forever!

Begin to preach God's prophetic Word. Begin to speak to your body and command it to come in line with the Word of God!

Just a few days after we finished those meetings in Spring Hill, Florida, Janet Angela and I traveled up to London, Ontario, Canada (my hometown), where we were given the opportunity to minister at the church where I had grown up. During the Sunday evening service I began to preach the Kingdom by making declarations of the things I knew God wanted to do in that church. I said something along the following lines:

"If you have back pain, I want you to come forward because God wants to release His healing power for you tonight!" (Back pain is always a great place to start with miracles because statistics show that over eighty percent of the world's population suffers from back problems!) "If you are having trouble with your eyes, I want you to come. If you have been losing your hearing, I want you to come."

I began prophesying to so many people's situations that we must have ended up with a line of fifty or sixty people in that small church! Do you know what happened that night?

The deaf began to hear, blurred vision became clear, those with back injuries and spine conditions received the healing flow of God's power. We witnessed one person after another give testimony to the healing power of God!

JESUS WAS DEMONSTRATING

> ***...and healing every sickness and every disease among the people.***
>
> – *Matthew 9:35 (KJV)*

We understand that Jesus was *teaching* the healing Word of God to the people, and Jesus was commanding healing miracles to come forth as he was *preaching* the prophetic Word of God, but now I want you to see that Jesus also began moving in the *demonstration* of these miracles. Whenever we teach healing and we preach the healing power of God, we must make room for the demonstration of that power to be revealed. The Apostle Paul boldly declared:

> ***And my speech and my preaching was not with enticing words of man's wisdom, but in demonstration of the Spirit and of power.***
> *– 1 Corinthians 2:4 (KJV)*

At the Intensified Glory Institute we always make an opportunity for each student to receive their healing miracles by demonstrating what has been taught and preached. As we have done this, we have witnessed some of the most outstanding miracles take place, which most likely would have never manifested if we hadn't made room for the miracles to happen.

We have experienced hundreds of backs being healed (both upper and lower back problems have completely disappeared); we have watched with our eyes as arms have grown out and legs have been lengthened. Sometimes the Holy Spirit has re-adjusted people's spines. Two times in particular people have actually grown taller at the Intensified Glory Institute as we have used our faith to press into this realm of the miraculous. Many people suffering from carpal tunnel have received instant healings. Brand new lungs and hearts have been created in this glory realm, hernias have disappeared, and the curse of various diseases has been broken off the lives of many. After teaching and preaching the healing power of God, you must make room to demonstrate this power. Many times you can do this by asking the person you're ministering to to do something they never could do before!

After preaching the healing power of God, we must make room to demonstrate this power!

- Jesus told the blind man to go wash his eyes. (John 9:7)
- Jesus told the crippled man to stand up and walk! (Matthew 9:6-7)
- Jesus told the lepers to go according to His word. (Luke 17:14)

These simple acts of faith become a point of contact for the miracles to be demonstrated!

> ***And it came to pass, that the father of Publius lay sick of a fever and of a bloody flux: to whom Paul entered in, and prayed, and laid his hands on him, and healed him. So when this was done, others also, which had diseases in the island, came, and were healed.***
>
> *– Acts 28:8-9 (KJV)*

At times people do not see the miracles because they haven't looked for them. It is important to always give opportunity for the miracles to be seen because this will also build faith in the hearts of others. When you teach and preach the Word, the Word will become alive and begin to manifest! Open your eyes and begin to look for the miracle. Do not look for the sickness. Do not look for the disease. Do not look for the pain. Look for the miracles and you will find them!

When you preach the Word, it becomes alive and begins to manifest!

News about him spread all over Syria, and people brought to him all who were ill with various diseases, those suffering severe pain, the demon-possessed, those having seizures, and the paralyzed, and he healed them.

– Matthew 4:24

Here are some keys to ministering God's healing power to the sick:

1. You must believe that healing is available today! (Hebrews 13:8)
2. Begin to teach the Word of God in regard to healing by speaking healing Scriptures. This will impart faith. (Romans 10:17)
3. Begin to preach the Word of God in regard to healing. Speak prophetically to the body and command it to line up with the Word of God. (Matthew 17:20)
4. Act on the Word and begin to do something you could not do before! This will release the visible manifestation. (James 1:22)

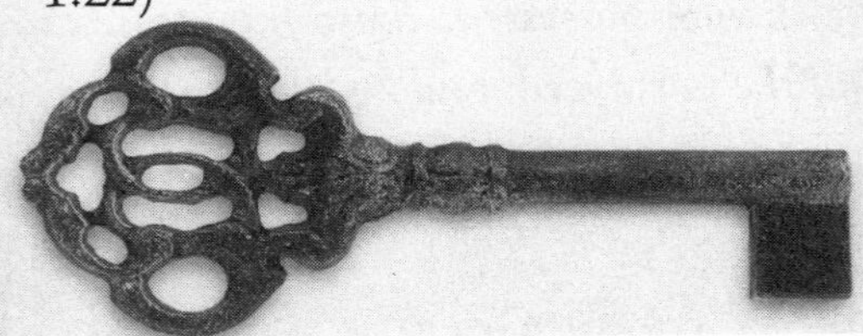

The following verses are some healing Scriptures to memorize, teach and preach as God uses you to minister healing to the sick .

(The following Scriptures are from the New Living Translation).

Exodus 15:26
He said, "If you will listen carefully to the voice of the Lord your God and do what is right in his sight, obeying his commands and keeping all his decrees, then I will not make you suffer any of the diseases I sent on the Egyptians; for I am the Lord who heals you."

Exodus 23:25-26
You must serve only the Lord your God. If you do, I will bless you with food and water, and I will protect you from illness. There will be no miscarriages or infertility in your land, and I will give you long, full lives.

Deuteronomy 7:15

And the Lord will protect you from all sickness. He will not let you suffer from the terrible diseases you knew in Egypt, but he will inflict them on all your enemies!

Psalm 67:2

May your ways be known throughout the earth, your saving power among people everywhere.

Psalm 91:9-10

If you make the Lord your refuge, if you make the Most High your shelter, no evil will conquer you; no plague will come near your home.

Psalm 103:1-5

Let all that I am praise the Lord; with my whole heart, I will praise his holy name. Let all that I am praise the Lord; may I never forget the good things he does for me. He forgives all my sins and heals all my diseases. He redeems me from death and crowns me with love and tender mercies. He fills my life with good things. My youth is renewed like the eagle's!

Psalm 107:19-20

"Lord, help!" they cried in their trouble, and he saved them from their distress. He sent out his word and healed them, snatching them from the door of death.

Psalm 118:17

I will not die; instead, I will live to tell what the Lord has done.

Proverbs 4:20-23

My child, pay attention to what I say. Listen carefully to my words. Don't lose sight of them. Let them penetrate deep into your heart, for they bring life to those who find them, and healing to their whole body. Guard your heart above all else, for it determines the course of your life.

Isaiah 41:10
Don't be afraid, for I am with you. Don't be discouraged, for I am your God. I will strengthen you and help you. I will hold you up with my victorious right hand.

Isaiah 53:4-5
Yet it was our weaknesses he carried; it was our sorrows that weighed him down. And we thought his troubles were a punishment from God, a punishment for his own sins! But he was pierced for our rebellion, crushed for our sins. He was beaten so we could be whole. He was whipped so we could be healed.

Isaiah 58:8
Then your salvation will come like the dawn, and your wounds will quickly heal. Your godliness will lead you forward, and the glory of the Lord will protect you from behind.

Isaiah 58:11
The Lord will guide you continually, giving you water when you are dry and restoring your strength. You will be like a well-watered garden, like an ever-flowing spring.

Jeremiah 30:17
"I will give you back your health and heal your wounds," says the Lord. "For you are called an outcast—'Jerusalem for whom no one cares.'"

Jeremiah 33:6
Nevertheless, the time will come when I will heal Jerusalem's wounds and give it prosperity and true peace.

Ezekiel 34:16

I will search for my lost ones who strayed away, and I will bring them safely home again. I will bandage the injured and strengthen the weak. But I will destroy those who are fat and powerful. I will feed them, yes—feed them justice!

Joel 3:10

Hammer your plowshares into swords and your pruning hooks into spears. Train even your weaklings to be warriors.

Malachi 3:6

I am the Lord, and I do not change. That is why you descendants of Jacob are not already destroyed.

Malachi 4:2

But for you who fear my name, the Sun of Righteousness will rise with healing in his wings. And you will go free, leaping with joy like calves let out to pasture.

Matthew 8:16
That evening many demon-possessed people were brought to Jesus. He cast out the evil spirits with a simple command, and he healed all the sick.

Matthew 9:35
Jesus traveled through all the towns and villages of that area, teaching in the synagogues and announcing the Good News about the Kingdom. And he healed every kind of disease and illness.

Matthew 15:30-31
A vast crowd brought to him people who were lame, blind, crippled, those who couldn't speak, and many others. They laid them before Jesus, and he healed them all. The crowd

was amazed! Those who hadn't been able to speak were talking, the crippled were made well, the lame were walking, and the blind could see again! And they praised the God of Israel.

Mark 11:22-24
Then Jesus said to the disciples, "Have faith in God. I tell you the truth, you can say to this mountain, 'May you be lifted up and thrown into the sea,' and it will happen. But you must really believe it will happen and have no doubt in your heart. I tell you, you can pray for anything, and if you believe that you've received it, it will be yours.

Mark 16:17-18
These miraculous signs will accompany those who believe: They will cast out demons in my name, and they will speak in new languages.

They will be able to handle snakes with safety, and if they drink anything poisonous, it won't hurt them. They will be able to place their hands on the sick, and they will be healed."

Luke 4:18-19

The Spirit of the Lord is upon me, for he has anointed me to bring Good News to the poor. He has sent me to proclaim that captives will be released, that the blind will see, that the oppressed will be set free, and that the time of the Lord's favor has come."

Luke 9:1-2

One day Jesus called together his twelve disciples and gave them power and authority to cast out all demons and to heal all diseases. Then he sent them out to tell everyone about the Kingdom of God and to heal the sick.

Luke 10:8-9

If you enter a town and it welcomes you, eat whatever is set before you. Heal the sick, and tell them, "The Kingdom of God is near you now."

John 10:10

The thief's purpose is to steal and kill and destroy. My purpose is to give them a rich and satisfying life.

Acts 4:29-30

And now, O Lord, hear their threats, and give us, your servants, great boldness in preaching your word. Stretch out your hand with healing power; may miraculous signs and wonders be done through the name of your holy servant Jesus.

Acts 5:15-16

As a result of the apostles' work, sick people were brought out into the streets on beds and mats so that Peter's shadow might fall across some of them as he went by. Crowds came from the villages around Jerusalem, bringing their sick and those possessed by evil spirits, and they were all healed.

Acts 10:38

And you know that God anointed Jesus of Nazareth with the Holy Spirit and with power. Then Jesus went around doing good and healing all who were oppressed by the devil, for God was with him.

Romans 8:11

The Spirit of God, who raised Jesus from the dead, lives in you. And just as God raised Christ Jesus from the dead, he will give life to your mortal bodies by this same Spirit living within you.

1 Thessalonians 5:23
Now may the God of peace make you holy in every way, and may your whole spirit and soul and body be kept blameless until our Lord Jesus Christ comes again.

Galatians 3:13
But Christ has rescued us from the curse pronounced by the law. When he was hung on the cross, he took upon himself the curse for our wrongdoing. For it is written in the Scriptures, "Cursed is everyone who is hung on a tree."

Philippians 2:13
For God is working in you, giving you the desire and the power to do what pleases him.

Philippians 4:6-7
Don't worry about anything; instead, pray about everything. Tell God what you need,

and thank him for all he has done. Then you will experience God's peace, which exceeds anything we can understand. His peace will guard your hearts and minds as you live in Christ Jesus.

James 5:13-16

Are any of you suffering hardships? You should pray. Are any of you happy? You should sing praises. Are any of you sick? You should call for the elders of the church to come and pray over you, anointing you with oil in the name of the Lord. Such a prayer offered in faith will heal the sick, and the Lord will make you well. And if you have committed any sins, you will be forgiven. Confess your sins to each other and pray for each other so that you may be healed. The earnest prayer of a righteous person has great power and produces wonderful results.

1 Peter 2:24

He personally carried our sins in his body on the cross so that we can be dead to sin and live for what is right. By his wounds you are healed.

1 John 5:14-15

And we are confident that he hears us whenever we ask for anything that pleases him. And since we know he hears us when we make our requests, we also know that he will give us what we ask for.

3 John 2

Dear friend, I hope all is well with you and that you are as healthy in body as you are strong in spirit.

Chapter Six

SEVEN KEYS TO THE GLORY REALM

In this chapter I'm going to share with you seven keys to the glory realm along with Scriptures that support each key.

1. FAITH IN JESUS CHRIST

While there are many ways to enter into the spirit realm, there is only one way into the realm of the glory – through faith in Jesus Christ. In order to access the glory realm, you MUST have faith in Jesus Christ!

(The following Scriptures are from the New Living Translation.)

Matthew 7:13-14
You can enter God's Kingdom only through the narrow gate. The highway to hell is broad, and its gate is wide for the many who choose that way. But the gateway to life is very narrow and the road is difficult, and only a few ever find it.

John 14:6
Jesus told him, "I am the way, the truth, and the life. No one can come to the Father except through me."

Galatians 3:26, 4:6-7
For you are all children of God through faith in Christ Jesus. And because we are his children, God has sent the Spirit of his Son into our hearts, prompting us to call out, "Abba,

Father." Now you are no longer a slave but God's own child. And since you are his child, God has made you his heir.

Romans 3:22
We are made right with God by placing our faith in Jesus Christ. And this is true for everyone who believes, no matter who we are.

Jesus is the ultimate manifestation of God's glory:

John 1:14
So the Word became human and made his home among us. He was full of unfailing love and faithfulness. And we have seen his glory, the glory of the Father's one and only Son.

2. Believe The Word Of God

We need to have a relationship with Him that goes beyond our natural sense realm and moves us into the "supernatural" sense realm of believing God's Word by faith. In order to walk in the glory realm, you must believe the Word of God!

> **John 20:27-31**
> ***Then he said to Thomas, "Put your finger here, and look at my hands. Put your hand into the wound in my side. Don't be faithless any longer. Believe!" "My Lord and my God!" Thomas exclaimed. Then Jesus told him, "You believe because you have seen me. Blessed are those who believe without seeing me." The disciples saw Jesus do many other miraculous signs in addition to the ones recorded in this book. But these are written so that you may continue to believe that Jesus is the Messiah, the Son of God, and that by believing in him you will have life by the power of his name.***

Believing the Word will cause you to live in the realm of glory:

> Psalm 37:3
> *Trust in the Lord and do good. Then you will live safely in the land and prosper.*

The "signs" or evidence of the glory realm will begin to manifest and follow you as you simply believe:

> Mark 16:15-20
> *And then he told them, "Go into all the world and preach the Good News to everyone. Anyone who believes and is baptized will be saved. But anyone who refuses to believe will be condemned. These miraculous signs will accompany those who believe: They will cast out demons in my name, and they will speak in new languages. They will be able to handle snakes with safety, and if they drink anything poisonous, it won't hurt them. They will be*

able to place their hands on the sick, and they will be healed." When the Lord Jesus had finished talking with them, he was taken up into heaven and sat down in the place of honor at God's right hand. And the disciples went everywhere and preached, and the Lord worked through them, confirming what they said by many miraculous signs.

Acts 2:42-47

All the believers devoted themselves to the apostles' teaching, and to fellowship, and to sharing in meals (including the Lord's Supper), and to prayer. A deep sense of awe came over them all, and the apostles performed many miraculous signs and wonders. And all the believers met together in one place and shared everything they had. They sold their property and possessions and shared the money with those in need. They worshiped together at the Temple each day, met in homes for the Lord's Supper, and shared their meals with great joy and generosity—all the while praising God and enjoying the goodwill of all the people. And each day the Lord added to their fellowship those who were being saved.

3. Unity, Honor, and Blessing

God desires for us to dwell together in unity:

John 17:20-26
I am praying not only for these disciples but also for all who will ever believe in me through their message. I pray that they will all be one, just as you and I are one—as you are in me, Father, and I am in you. And may they be in us so that the world will believe you sent me. I have given them the glory you gave me, so they may be one as we are one. I am in them and you are in me. May they experience such perfect unity that the world will know that you sent me and that you love them as much

as you love me. Father, I want these whom you have given me to be with me where I am. Then they can see all the glory you gave me because you loved me even before the world began! O righteous Father, the world doesn't know you, but I do; and these disciples know you sent me. I have revealed you to them, and I will continue to do so. Then your love for me will be in them, and I will be in them.

Psalm 133:1-3

How wonderful and pleasant it is when brothers live together in harmony! For harmony is as precious as the anointing oil that was poured over Aaron's head, that ran down his beard and onto the border of his robe. Harmony is as refreshing as the dew from Mount Hermon that falls on the mountains of Zion. And there the Lord has pronounced his blessing, even life everlasting.

Romans 15:5-6

May God, who gives this patience and encouragement, help you live in complete harmony with each other, as is fitting for followers of Christ Jesus. Then all of you can join together with one voice, giving praise and glory to God, the Father of our Lord Jesus Christ.

God wants us to honor those around us – our fathers and mothers, and those who have gone before us in the faith:

Deuteronomy 5:16

Honor your father and mother, as the Lord your God commanded you. Then you will live a long, full life in the land the Lord your God is giving you.

Bless those around you:

> **Genesis 12:3**
> ***I will bless those who bless you and curse those who treat you with contempt. All the families on earth will be blessed through you.***

4. Holiness, Righteousness, and Humility

The Bible speaks about the "Highway of Holiness" and that we are called to be a "peculiar people" (KJV) set apart for the purposes of God. As we ask the Lord to visit us with this anointing of holiness, righteousness, and humility, we will receive an impartation that will cause us to access the glory realm at a greater degree than ever before:

> **Isaiah 35:8**
> ***And a great road will go through that once deserted land. It will be named the Highway of Holiness. Evil-minded people will never travel on it. It will be only for those who walk in God's ways; fools will never walk there.***

1 Peter 2:9

But you are not like that, for you are a chosen people. You are royal priests, a holy nation, God's very own possession. As a result, you can show others the goodness of God, for he called you out of the darkness into his wonderful light.

We must come before the Lord with humility:

Philippians 2:5-11

You must have the same attitude that Christ Jesus had. Though he was God, he did not think of equality with God as something to cling to. Instead, he gave up his divine privileges; he took the humble position of a slave and was born as a human being. When he appeared in human form, he humbled himself in obedience to God and died a criminal's death on a cross. Therefore, God elevated him to the place of highest honor and gave him the name above all other names, that at the name of Jesus every knee should bow, in heaven and on earth and under the earth, and every tongue confess that Jesus Christ is Lord, to the glory of God the Father.

Proverbs 22:4
True humility and fear of the Lord lead to riches, honor, and long life.

Luke 14:11
For those who exalt themselves will be humbled, and those who humble themselves will be exalted.

5. Do Not Be Moved by Persecutions

We are blessed during times of persecution that have been caused for His name's sake. We will receive heavenly treasures and rewards when others attempt to persecute us!

Matthew 5:10-12

God blesses those who are persecuted for doing right, for the Kingdom of Heaven is theirs. God blesses you when people mock you and persecute you and lie about you and say all sorts of evil things against you because you are my followers. Be happy about it! Be very glad! For a great reward awaits you in heaven. And remember, the ancient prophets were persecuted in the same way.

Luke 6:22-23

What blessings await you when people hate you and exclude you and mock you and curse you as evil because you follow the Son of Man. When that happens, be happy! Yes, leap for joy! For a great reward awaits you in heaven. And remember, their ancestors treated the ancient prophets that same way.We need to bless those who persecute us:

Romans 12:14
Bless those who persecute you. Don't curse them; pray that God will bless them.

6. Praise and Worship

Your praise changes the atmosphere and your worship sustains that realm! Praise and worship are the keys that unlock the pathway into the glory realm. We enter into His presence with praise.

Psalm 100:1
Shout with joy to the Lord, all the earth!

1 Thessalonians 5:16, 18
Always be joyful. Be thankful in all circumstances, for this is God's will for you who belong to Christ Jesus.

Isaiah 61:11

The Sovereign Lord will show his justice to the nations of the world. Everyone will praise him! His righteousness will be like a garden in early spring, with plants springing up everywhere.

Isaiah 45:8

Open up, O heavens, and pour out your righteousness. Let the earth open wide so salvation and righteousness can sprout up together. I, the Lord, created them.

7. Generosity

Your generosity opens up a realm of blessing, favor, and increase that causes the abundance of heaven's bounty to fill your life! If we want to imitate the example of Christ, we must learn how to be generous. John 3:16 tells us that God so loved the world that He gave!

Deuteronomy 16:17
All must give as they are able, according to the blessings given to them by the Lord your God.

Proverbs 3:9
Honor the Lord with your wealth and with the best part of everything you produce.

2 Corinthians 9:6
Remember this—a farmer who plants only a few seeds will get a small crop. But the one who plants generously will get a generous crop.

Luke 6:38
Give, and you will receive. Your gift will return to you in full—pressed down, shaken together to make room for more, running over, and poured into your lap. The amount you give will determine the amount you get back.

Acts 20:35
And I have been a constant example of how you can help those in need by working hard. You should remember the words of the Lord Jesus: 'It is more blessed to give than to receive.'"

Remember that we are supposed to live from the dimension of the glory realm. In the glory realm we will produce greater results. Put these seven keys into practice and flow in the glory realm. In the glory, God will produce a greater harvest through us as we yield to His Word and His ways.

Chapter Seven

The Commission

In the Word of God, Jesus Christ gives His disciples a commission. If you have accepted Jesus Christ as your Lord and Savior, then you are a disciple of Christ and He is commissioning you too! I want you to read this passage of Scripture, and as you do, listen to what Jesus Christ is saying to you today through His Word.

> ***He said to them, "Go into all the world and preach the good news to all creation. Whoever believes and is baptized will be saved, but whoever does not believe will be condemned. And these signs will accompany***

> ***those who believe: In my name they will drive out demons; they will speak in new tongues; they will pick up snakes with their hands; and when they drink deadly poison, it will not hurt them at all; they will place their hands on sick people, and they will get well." After the Lord Jesus had spoken to them, he was taken up into heaven and he sat at the right hand of God. Then the disciples went out and preached everywhere, and the Lord worked with them and confirmed his word by the signs that accompanied it."***
>
> *– Mark 16:15-20*

Through this Scripture Jesus tells us to "GO into all the world." I want you to realize that Jesus didn't say to stay put, fasten your seatbelt, or to be comfortable in the church pew. He said to "Go!" This is the commission that He is giving you today. Jesus even said that you would do greater miracles than He did on the earth!

Verily, verily, I say unto you, He that believeth on me, the works that I do shall he do also; and greater works than these shall he do; because I go unto my Father.

– John 14:12 (KJV)

As you have read this book, I pray that you have felt the anointing of God filling you with His strength for supernatural soul winning, the baptism in the Holy Spirit, and the ability to go forth and heal the sick.

Now, I give you my blessing to... Go and do it!!!

This is simple supernatural!

But don't just listen to God's word. You must do what it says. Otherwise, you are only fooling yourselves. *– James 1:22 (NLT)*

JOSHUA MILLS

An anointed minister of the gospel, recording artist, conference speaker and author, Joshua Mills worships and preaches by standing under the cloud and ministering directly from the glory unto the people. He has written over 600 songs and is known for his ability to lead people into spontaneous worship.

Traveling all over North America and around the world, he has been creating a realm of glory wherever he goes, with a clear message that "praise changes the atmosphere."

Along with holding meetings in Europe, South America, Asia, Australia, New Zealand, and other nations, Joshua Mills has ministered extensively throughout the Canadian Arctic regions witnessing dramatic transformation taking place in whole communities and in the lives of many Inuit people.

Author contact info:

New Wine International, Inc.
Phone: 1-866-60-NEW-WINE
Online: www.NewWineInternational.org

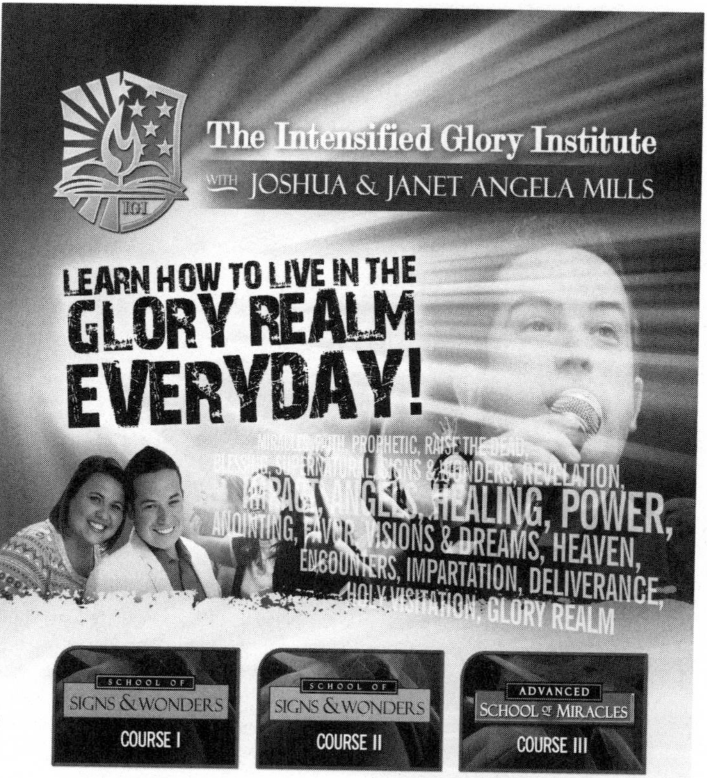

TRANSFORM YOUR SPIRITUAL LIFE IN 14-DAYS

with the School Of Signs & Wonders, Home Study Course!

IGI
The Intensified Glory Institute

GREAT FOR...

personal home study, cell groups, Sunday Schools, bible studies and church leadership training!

In this school Joshua Mills will share keys with you that will unlock God's supernatural overflow in your life. You will discover the following topics: The Three Realms of the Supernatural, How To Hear God's Voice, Exploring The Realms of Heavenly Glory, How To Operate In Creative Miracles, Activating Angels, Transport In The Spirit, The Power Of Praise & Worship, Miraculous Blessing, Third Day Intercession, Flowing In Unusual Signs & Wonders ...plus more!

This special School Of Signs & Wonders, Home Study Course comes in a beautiful full-color display box and includes 1 Student Manual, 2 full-color study charts, 14-DVD library collection featuring almost twenty hours of teaching, plus so much more...

Are you ready to go to the next level? Order Yours Today!

Call toll-free: 1-866-60-NEW-WINE

Online 24/7: www.NewWineInternational.org

Joshua & Janet Angela Mills' Glory Resources

Teaching CDs

Childbirth In The Glory

Glory & Grace

Heavenly Things: Throne Room Encounters

May I Bless You?

Ministering With Angels: How To Activate The Angelic Realm In Your Life

Miracle Money

Praise Changes The Atmosphere

Simple Supernatural

The Power Of Praise

The Power Of The Glory Cloud

The Power Of Your Testimony

Translation & Heaven's Transportation

Music CDs

Holy Invasion: Live From Hollywood, California

Let's Get High

Let's Get High (Ministry Version)

Let's Get High (Performance Trax)

SpiritSpa: Piano Instrumental

SpiritSpa 2

The Drink

Waterfall

Teaching Manuals & Songbooks

Childbirth In The Glory: Declarations & Prayers

IGI School Of Signs & Wonders – Course I

IGI School Of Signs & Wonders – Course II

IGI Advanced School Of Miracles – Course III

Into His Presence: Praise & Worship Manual

Personal Ministry Prayer Manual

Waterfall Songbook

Dear Friend,

I believe that you are a kingdom connection! God wants to use you to make a difference in the lives of thousands around the world. Do you believe that?

I would like to invite you to become a ***Partner in Praise*** with me, and help me take this supernatural message of Jesus Christ and His glory to the far corners of the earth.

Partnership is not simply giving of your finances; it is more. When you become a ***Partner in Praise*** with this ministry, you will become an integral member of the New Wine International outreach ministry team with special opportunities and privileges that will position you to have global impact.

A ***"Partner in Praise"*** is a person who agrees to:

1. Financially support the ministry of New Wine International (NWI)
2. Pray faithfully for Joshua & Janet Angela Mills and the NWI Ministry Team as they carry the message of Jesus Christ around the world.
3. Pray for those who will receive ministry through NWI ministry events and resources.

Partnership is not only what you can do to help me, but also what I can do to help you. Becoming a ***Partner in Praise*** with N.W.I. provides a covenant agreement between you and me. By being a ***Partner in Praise,*** you will connect with the anointing and glory on this ministry as I send you monthly updates and revelatory teachings on the glory realm. You will receive my continued prayer for you and your family and you will be linked with the unique anointing that is on this ministry for unusual signs and wonders.

There are currently several ways to partner with NWI. I want you to decide the partnership level according to what the Lord has placed in your heart to do.

In His Great Love,

Joshua Mills

P.S. *Call my office today to become a partner or register online so that I can send you a special* ***Partners In Praise*** *Welcome Package filled with special benefits and information.*

Toll-Free: **1-866-60-NEW-WINE**
Online 24/7: **www.NewWineInternational.org**
www.PartnersInPraise.com

To order more copies of *Simple Supernatural* please visit the store at newwineinternational.org or call: 1-866-60-NEW-WINE (1-866-606-3994)

You may also order more copies of *Simple Supernatural* and other books from XP Publishing at the store at XPmedia.com

BULK ORDERS: We have bulk/wholesale prices for stores and ministries. Please contact: usaresource@xpmedia.com.

For Canadian bulk orders please contact: resource@xpmedia.com or call 250-765-9286.

XPpublishing.com
A ministry of Christian Services Association